The 'Not So Secret' Diary of a Midlife Menopausal Mum

By

Katie Taylor

Text copyright @ November 2017

Katie Taylor

All Rights Reserved by

Katie Taylor

Published by Satin Publishing

Cover & Illustrations by: Michael Baum

© 2017, Katie Taylor, except as provided by the Copyright Act January 2015 no part of this publication may be reproduced, stored in a retrieval system or transmitted in any form or by any means without the prior written permission of the Author and Publisher.

ISBN-13: 978-1983888649
ISBN-10: 1983888648

Author Biography

 Katie has worked for the past 25 years in PR, Marketing, Fundraising and Event Organising for a variety of charities, helping children and adults with learning disabilities, seriously ill children and teenagers in hospital, as well as supporting adults with mental health problems.

She set up the Facebook Group 'The Latte Lounge' to help women over 40 with all mid-life issues. The new website is an extension to this group, and for members to access more detailed information than they can otherwise on the group page.

This is her first book; a collection of humorous and poignant blogs that she originally wrote for the group.

Background to the Latte Lounge Facebook Group and this book

A few years ago, aged 45, I had just returned to work after a long break bringing up my four children. I loved my life, but for no reason that I could fathom, I was feeling exhausted, teary and down. My GP diagnosed what he thought was depression and prescribed anti-depressants. This, it turned out, was a misdiagnosis.

After six months, I felt worse. I had 'brain fog', couldn't think clearly at work, cried at the most inconvenient moments, and then didn't want to leave my house.

I stopped socialising with my friends or speaking on the phone to anyone, and piled on an enormous amounts of weight. The anti-depressants turned me into a zombie, I felt nothing — it just wasn't right.

I feared it was the pressure of combining home-life with a demanding job. After all, I had so much to do; moving house, settling one child into university and nurturing the others through exams.

So, I spoke to my father, Professor Michael Baum, who is an eminent Breast Cancer specialist, and very knowledgeable in all areas of women's health, and asked what he thought I should do. He suggested I seek a second opinion from one of his colleagues at the University College Hospital, because despite my age, he thought I could be menopausal.

And it turned out that he was right. I was deep in the throes of peri-menopause. The consultant and I agreed I should start HRT; a combined oestrogen and progesterone pill and wean myself off the anti-depressants slowly.

For the first month I didn't notice a huge change, although I definitely felt my mood lighten. But, after about a month, I suddenly noticed a massive difference — it was like I had got the old Katie back.

It was at this point that I had the idea of starting up a Facebook group. I found there were many groups out there talking about bringing up young children, but nothing much for older women.

So I decided to create a 2D coffee shop for mid-life women to share their tips, support, recommendations, advice, and news articles and the name "The Latte Lounge (Top tips 4 Women Over 40!) was conceived.

We talk about everything, from healthy eating to hot flushes, Brexit to breast screening. Most of all, we discuss the dilemma of looking after ourselves, while also caring for teenage children and ageing parents. Our group is for women-only, a closed and safe space for us to confide in each other.

It has been the best kind of therapy for me; it has made me realise that I am not alone and that, actually, going through menopause is completely normal. What I've learnt is that too many of us suffer in silence and don't seek help. Or we do, but get the wrong diagnosis. There is still such a taboo, and many women feel they have no one to talk to.

Last year, I organised two "Latte Lounge" retreat days to raise money and awareness. One was for Ovarian Cancer Action and the other for The Daisy Network which supports women suffering from early menopause. I also organised a group auction for Chai Cancer Care, which was an enormous success.

So the next step in the growth of the group seemed like a very natural phase; the creation of *The Latte Lounge website*, a place to go where perhaps a bit more detail is needed for members to access.

I also hope to set up a charity with my father, in the not too distant future, which will link the Facebook Group and Website together, so that we can raise money for all areas of Women's Health.

This book is a collection of some of my Mid-life extracts/blogs that have been posted on the Facebook Group over the past year. They are quite personal and poignant at times, but always laced with a lot of humour and positivity that I hope you will all be able to enjoy and relate to on some level.

Thank you for reading.

Acknowledgements

The inspiration behind setting up an online support group for women, came from my fond memory of my grandma Mary Baum who passed away from Breast Cancer far too early, and to honour the lifetimes selfless work of finding a cure for Breast Cancer by her son, and my father, Professor Michael Baum.

It is also a thanks to my lovely Mum, who has always stood by his side and supported him throughout.

Dedications

This book is dedicated to my amazing and long suffering husband Hugh and my four beautiful children; Ellie, Josh, Sam and Joe.

And, my adorable Cavachon pup, Bobbie.

AUTHOR LINKS:

https://www.thesun.co.uk/fabulous/4666261/menopause-last-taboo-sex-lives-worries-health/

http://lifewiselady.com/25-facebook-groups-midlifers-boomers/

http://www.britmums.com/2016/10/facebook-groups-aimed-mums/

https://www.thejc.com/landing/Author/Katie%20Taylor

https://www.aftertheplayground.com/blogs-for-mums-of-teens/

SOCIAL MEDIA LINKS

Twitter: @Lounge_Latte

Facebook: https://www.facebook.com/groups/250120855345911/

The Latte Lounge (Top Tips 4 Women over 40!)

Instagram: @Loungethelatte

Publisher Links:

http://www.satinpublishing.co.uk

https://twitter.com/SatinPaperbacks

https://www.facebook.com/Satinpaperbacks.com

Email: nicky.fitzmaurice@satinpublishing.co.uk

Table of Contents:

JANUARY 2017 – HORMONES FLUCTUATE AS THE KIDS GROW UP AND I GROW OUT!......1

That Green Dress..1

Oh To Be 21 Again! 8

FEBRUARY 2017 – LET'S GET A DOG 12

What's Apping Gone Wrong....................................12

The Postman...15

Dog Walking Stress..17

MARCH 2017 – TV, TEENS & TALKING.............20

Boys Talk 20

Cycling Free! 23

APRIL 2017 – GRANDPARENTS HIT THE NET .27

An Old Recipe With A Difference 27

MAY 2017 – FITNESS FADS...................................34

50 Shades of Exercise 34

JUNE 2017 – BACK TO WORK 36

'It's A Whole New World'..36

JULY 2017 – SOMETHING'S MISSING! 39

Where's my keys, where's my car, where's my memory?..39

AUGUST 2017 – HOLIDAY AT SEA......................42

An Alternative View On Cruising, By a Virgin Cruiser 42

Cruise Day 3 45

Last Day At Sea 46
SEPTEMBER 2017 – FAREWELL DEAR
WOMB 48
Hysterical Hysterectomy 48
OCTOBER 2017 – BACK TO THE FUTURE 58
Can We Talk Retro? 58
NOVEMBER 2017 – MEN HUH? 61
Whoaaaa! 61
Husband Trade-Off 64
DECEMBER 2017 – RIGHT ON WOMEN 66
Putting The Feminine Back In Feminism 66
*THE LATTE LOUNGE FACEBOOK GROUP 2017
YEAR IN REVIEW* 70

JANUARY 2017 – HORMONES FLUCTUATE AS THE KIDS GROW UP AND I GROW OUT!

That Green Dress

Forget My Big Fat Greek Wedding,
Move Over Bridget Jones' Diary,
Make Way For...
My Big Fat Jewish 3 Month Barmitzvah Diary!

3 months, 3 stone and 3 dresses later, why has the pressure of finding the perfect dress caused me to be sitting here crying over my laptop with a week to go before my youngest son, Joe's Barmitzvah?

Well, to answer that question, I need to take you back a few months to when I went to see my GP. It seemed the right thing to do as I had piled on a load of weight, was feeling blue, tired and spaced out all the time, and was now panicking about looking and feeling good, not just for the Barmitzvah, but also for my own mental and physical health.

Anyway, after lots of different checks and tests, I ask the question:

Dr, am I going mad? Apparently not.
Am I having a mid-life crisis? Nope.
Am I depressed? Definitely Not.

So what the heck is wrong with me?

After all, what have I got to complain about? I am so fortunate; I have a wonderful hubby, 4 fab kids, a beautiful house and the luxury of working from home, so, supposedly, I have the perfect work/life balance. Shouldn't I therefore be walking on air, shouting from the rooftops, laughing at all my friends jokes as they try to cheer me up?

"Well yes, but not at the moment," she replies. "It's simple," she says, "it's your hormones."

"My Hor-mones," I moan (pardon the pun!) "What have they got to do with anything?"

"Well," she said, "your blood tests show that you have very low oestrogen and iron levels. Which means you are anaemic and you are pretty much entering the next 'chapter' of your life – the MENOPAUSE.

The anaemia is very easy to sort out with daily iron tablets. As for the hormones, well that'll take a bit more time, but I can definitely help you."

So, after a half-hour conversation with her recommending everything from natural remedies to HRT, diet and exercise plans, we decided that I should just enjoy my summer holiday and then come back and gently start getting myself into some sort of shape.

Ok, that was the plan then. So I bought a lovely stretchy dress in America to wear for the big day, no matter what the scales would say, and when I got home I put it away and happily carried on with my life. But then all those holiday ice creams, and all my children's birthday parties and suddenly it's 4 weeks to go and Shittttttttttt! My dress I'd bought in America, for some reason doesn't quite stretch as much as I had thought it would.

Ok, calm… It's only a dress, no biggie. It was cheap anyway, I can sell it on Ebay, there's still plenty of time.

So off I go to Westfield with hubby and his ever decreasing wallet by my side and 3 hours later, just as we were about to give up hope, the perfect green dress was found. With utter relief and happiness, I put it safely away as soon as I get home and I'm all relaxed again, knowing that at least the clothing situation was now sorted.

Or, so I thought…

10 days to go and I start laying out all my clothes; working out what shoes will go with what bag, what hat with what dress. I suddenly look over at my new green dress and feel a rise of panic slowly creeping up my body. WTF is that? Why TF did I buy that?

Shittttttttttt! I hate it, it looks like something that belongs in my fridge, hidden somewhere between the over-ripe aubergine, avocado and cucumbers!

By this time, my husband threatens to leave me if I even mention the word 'dress' again. So, after 2 terrible sleepless nights, I decide there's only one thing for it. I'm going to form a relationship with Asos, Boohoo and The Outnet and my new boyfriend Malcolm, (yes, we are on first name terms now!) at the Post Office counter in the High Street.

I spend that night trawling through hundreds of

online items that all look incredible, and even better when they are discounted by 75%. Hour by hour the parcels start arriving, and I tell myself that it's all ok, because I'm sending all but one back, so my husband will never know as my credit card will be credited back within 24 hours. There was blue, pink , purple, orange, spots, stripes, checks, lace, satin, sequins, maxi, mini – you name it, I tried it.

But here's the problem with this sort of shopping experience. Firstly, and this may come as a surprise to many of you, but I am not a blonde, 6ft tall, 21 year old model with perfectly toned and suntanned legs. I am sadly a semi-permanent brown dyed, 5ft 4 inch, 47 year old woman with perfectly lumpy pale and badly shaven legs!

So basically, what looks like catwalk heaven online, in reality looks like something out of a horror show. However, I do finally find something that seems to hide all the lumps and bumps and I settle on a little (well large) black cocktail dress. I tell myself that, 'I will simply just merge into the background with the other 100 women all in short black cocktail dresses,' after all, who cares? No one is looking at me, it's all about my little boy becoming a man.

I pack everything back up, run down to the Post Office for the 8th time that day, hand over the dresses to my new best friend, Malcolm, and with a sigh of relief wave them off praying that the credit will show sooner than my husband noticing we've had some 'unusual activity' on our bank account.

And that brings us neatly up to today, and why I'm sitting here crying over my laptop.

I'm not crying because I'm sad, I'm crying with happiness and relief because my gorgeous, long suffering hubby, and a couple of wonderful friends of mine said something really special to me yesterday.

"You are a beautiful woman inside and out. You may not be the weight you would like to be, you may not like the way you look when you see yourself in the mirror, but no-one else sees or thinks about that, we all love you because you are you.

You should not be wearing a little black dress and hiding in the shadows, you should put on a bright coloured dress and dazzle us with your smile and your love of your family, because life is too short to hide and black is for funerals, not for celebrating a wonderful family occasion."

So guess what? I didn't lose a single pound in 3 months, both in terms of weight or actually in terms of money, but I did go back to that green dress, and after trying it on just now – I actually do quite like it, even if I do resemble a vegetable!

Therefore, next weekend, I will try and wear it with pride and confidence and enjoy every second, because you only get one life and I want to enjoy it.

(I have to say though, I will definitely miss seeing Malcolm so often, but I've promised to write!)

Oh, and as for HRT? Well that can wait a few weeks.

Oh To Be 21 Again!

My beautiful, clever, funny, kind and giving daughter, as clichéd as it may sound, is also my best friend.

It's Saturday night, and instead of being out at my daughters 21st birthday party, I'm at home in front of my computer... blubbing (again!).

This time not over a green dress but over the sight of her and feeling a deep, emotional pain that I just can't explain.

She didn't want a big party tonight with lots of family and friends, speeches, dancing and presents, she hates having all that attention on her. So she's gone out for dinner and to a bar with her friends and that's great – and frankly saves me a fortune and the aggro of looking for another green dress!

But I guess I'm blubbing because, deep down, I have to admit I would've quite liked to have partied with her, and then perhaps done a little speech tonight and told her how proud I am of the woman she has become, and how lucky I am to have her in my life.

She was born a year and a half after my first pregnancy, which had ended in a miscarriage. She certainly healed our wounds and we named her Eliana (Ellie for short), because it meant God has answered our prayers, and he/she (let's not get all gender neutral here right now!) really did.

When others complained of the toddler tantrums and the teenage arguments, I smiled and pretended to nod knowingly, but secretly I thanked my lucky stars this was not my experience. Never an argument or a cross word; she was mature and grown up from the minute her first brother Josh was born 21 months later.

Perhaps it's because she would go on to be the oldest of 4 kids, all under the age of 7 years old, my big girl helper I'd call her. I often felt guilty for not having the time I would have loved to devote to my only daughter, but I was just so swamped in babies and toddlers and nappies and boy tantrums, it was never an option. But she never once complained, she took it all in her stride.

No wonder she's studying psychology at Uni. If anyone can figure out what makes toddlers tick, or what makes a young mum an emotional wreck, it's her!

No wonder she is surrounded by so many amazing friends who constantly go to her for advice.

No wonder she has a devoted boyfriend, who is always by her side.

No wonder she lights up a room whenever she walks in and always manages to make us all laugh.

No wonder she has always mothered me when I've not been feeling well.

And it is no wonder her room is a complete mess and her table manners are really quite questionable – there you go, no-ones that perfect! (After all, I never had the time to teach her!)

I look at her at 21 and it takes my breath away. Where has the time gone, where has my baby girl gone? As I enter my 50th year it has been a rude awakening; Where has my youth gone? I feel fat, frumpy, dull and old next to this smiley, shiny, beautiful, bubbly, breath of fresh air with a figure to die for.

But it's not all tears. I'm also incredibly happy tonight. Seeing her all grown up, I know we have done a good job and I have to stand back and watch her fly.

I also know how incredibly lucky and blessed I am to have children full stop, when for so many others they have not been as lucky, and after experiencing the heartache of my own first miscarriage, I have never once taken it for granted.

So as I sit here tonight and look through all the old photos of her growing up, I know that this kind of emotional pain of LOVE is something that I never want to find a cure for.

And tomorrow, as I pack her off for her final year of Uni, I will pledge to make more time for me, to perhaps try and turn back the clock just a little bit and get this middle-aged woman back to something vaguely resembling her 21 year old self! (Well I'll be happy with 41 to be honest!)

FEBRUARY 2017 – LET'S GET A DOG

What's Apping Gone Wrong

OMG kill me now! I have made such a mess and all simply with a touch of the "Send" key!

You see, 6 months ago I entered a new, unfamiliar and slightly scary world. The world of searching for a new puppy.

My kids have been desperate for one for the last 10 years, but with four kids under the age of 7 and having always been a bit scared of dogs myself, I had to wait until the time was right.

Fast forward ten years and the time is now right, what with my oldest away at Uni and my no 2 at College, the house seems slightly quieter and there is a small aching hole that needs to be filled. And then of course, there's the growing desire to get out much more and walk every day in the fresh air.

But wow, I wasn't expecting this minefield of madness. What happened to the days of going to a pet shop?

Anyway, after months of conversations to find the right breed, we had all finally settled on a Cavachon, as frankly who can resist those big brown eyes and with child no 3 allergic to shedding fur, it was a good hypoallergenic breed for us.

I learnt so many new terms during my search and apparently I was after an F1, Blenheim Cavachon bitch (rude!)

Anyway, after 6 months of chatting with our chosen breeder, it was all going swimmingly well. Right up that is until yesterday, when I accidentally sent a What's App message which was meant solely for our family group, but instead I sent it to the potential breeder saying I was having a few (menopausal induced anxiety) doubts, and were they all 100% sure about this puppy?

On the back of that, the breeder, who loves her puppies more than her own children said if I was having doubts, then she would always be worried and it was best we don't continue. So now, after 6 months of painstaking research, I have lost the pup we had set ourselves up for at the next month and far worse, my kids are now not talking to me!!

Note to self: get rid of What's App groups and let rational husband make all important decisions from now on!

(Ps. It's funny. Now that I've lost the pup, I've never been more sure in my life that it is exactly what I want!) Anyone got an F1 Blenheim Cavachon bitch for sale?

The Postman

I can never, ever, ever go into my local newsagent ever again. Actually scrap that, I need to move country NOW!

You see, we have a glass panel on our front door, right above the letterbox and at 5.50am today, as I was just about to jump into the shower, our puppy, (yes, I did manage to sweet talk the breeder into eventually changing her mind!) started crying to be let out at the back door which is across the hall, directly opposite the front door.

So, it is at that exact time, as I run in my 47 year old birthday suit to let her out, that our newsagent decides to post the morning's newspapers through the door.

It would've been pretty embarrassing for him to have just caught a glimpse of my rather, for want of a better word, 'voluptuous' backside, but NO, I stupidly decided to turn right around as I hear the letterbox clang, and there he was- so what do I do?

Any normal woman would scream and run upstairs, but oh no not me; I smiled, waved and shouted Morning! (WTF? Who does that?!)

Then I remembered what I wasn't wearing and with

only two hands, what's a girl to cover? I scarpered.

OMG! I feel sick, think it's time to get a new front door!

Dog Walking Stress

'Get a dog', they said. 'You'll walk everyday', they said. 'Be great for destressing', they said.

'It'll get lost in the woods for half an hour and you will come home with your nerves and your sanity in shreds', they didn't say.

'Bobbie Come!' usually works a treat, with a treat in hand that is. But oh no, not today.

Bobbie most certainly didn't come; not when I screamed my lungs off for half an hour, not when my husband casually called her name in a very monosyllabic 'I'm too masculine to show that I'm actually crapping myself that this beautiful ball of fluff that I pretend I don't love is never coming home and has been eaten by a fox, stolen by the local dog catcher or trapped with a broken limb in some wired fencing far off in the distance' kinda way.

My stress levels were rising to a level of panic I haven't experienced since that time I lost my oldest son 17 years ago, aged 2 for 30 seconds whilst he quietly exited a sandpit and wandered off as I was turning around to put my rubbish in a bin, only to be found happily playing halfway up a nearby tree.

So what does one do in this situation when your

puppy, who you thought had perfectly nailed the recall side of training, doesn't recall what to do (i.e. come back?)

Well, obviously you type into Google on your iPhone the words 'noises to play on YouTube to get a lost dog to come back to you'. You see, the noise I played sounded like a cross between a howling wolf and my toilet being flushed. The resulting consequence was;

(a.) my husband screaming at me that he really did think I had finally lost the plot and,

(b.) who knew that it was the perfect way to attract a family of squirrels to your side?

But... who loves squirrels more than me? More than treats? More than obeying her recall training? Bobbie!! So... not so crazy after all, huh?

She was finally back with a vengeance! And all at the sight and sound of 15 squirrels who I now know are apparently attracted to the sounds of a wolf being flushed down a toilet.

So, my relaxing country walk may have resulted in my heart rate being pushed up to a level beyond which no middle-aged woman should ever be pushed, but I've learnt something new and now I'm thinking of creating an App for owners of lost dogs called the WOLFLUSH.

MARCH 2017 – TV, TEENS & TALKING
Boys Talk

I often hear my friends and many women say they wish their teenagers, boys in particular, would talk to them, or that they've no idea what's going on in their lives/heads, etc.

I also have many friends who have the same issue with their daughters, although not in my case. In fact, sometimes I wish she'd stop telling me how many times she's been to the toilet that day!

Well, I have a solution after watching the TV programme 'I'm a celebrity get me out of here!' With two of my teenage boys, let me tell you, it's definitely the way forward.

Yes, many people may sneer and say it's such garbage TV, or perhaps some of you may love it, but as far as I'm concerned, right now it's the best thing on TV because last night, for almost two hours, it gave us the opportunity to sit together and talk in a natural environment.

We laughed at the mostly Z list Celebs, we talked about what we did and didn't like about each of their personalities, and why and whether we would do certain challenges. Then, in the breaks, they carried on talking about their own lives; issues, innermost thoughts and dreams, both to me and each other without once looking at their phones.

I've always found the best way to talk to my boys is in a car, or cinema, or walking somewhere in a non-threatening way, i.e. no eye contact, looking straight ahead, casually chatting as if I'm not bothered either way, but secretly thrilled that they are drip feeding their thoughts to me.

And FYI, I actually love watching 'I'm a celebrity get me out of here!' anyway, not because of the Z-listers, but because I have a secret crush(;) I LOVE the hosts, Ant 'n Dec. There I said it, it's out, I don't care, they make me laugh, what can I say.

So, for the next 3 weeks, I'm on a mission to gain as much top secret info as I can from my boys, before it's too late and they retreat back into their bedrooms never to be seen until next year's programme!

Cycling Free!

"I'm always happy when I'm here, Mum," says my 14 year old son, as we stop on our bikes to gaze at the beautiful lake in front of us.

"Me too," I sigh, as we both stand in silence breathing in the cold, fresh air and smell of the pine trees in the forest, quietly waiting for the others to catch up with us.

Ok, so I don't mean to start this blog like the beginning of a very twee Enid Blyton book, but I promise you that was exactly how the scene and conversation unfolded that morning!

"Why do you think you love it so much?" I asked, expecting him to shrug his shoulders in his usual teenage monosyllabic manner and mumble "Dunno" under his breath.

"Because I get away from all the social crap and the phone constantly beeping and the pressure from the teachers at school to conform and behave and I love feeling free with no homework."

"Wow!" I say, quite stunned at him being able to pinpoint exactly what I was pretty much feeling too.

Centre Parcs has become a firm family favourite of ours over the last decade, it's certainly not the cheapest holiday in England, but for us it's the easiest and most enjoyable way to have a family break together regardless of the kids ages. It's the simplicity of life that each of us loves and for whatever reason, there are no arguments.

A cosy cabin in the middle of a forest, at the edge of a lake, surrounded by all manners of natural wildlife. Our only transport being by bike, gives even the youngest of kids the chance to experience what real freedom feels like.

A typical day usually includes playing badminton in the indoor sporting hall, followed by a long cycle ride before having some lunch in the lakeside pancake house. We would cycle back to our cabin and chill for a bit in front of a real log fire and play cards, maybe watch TV or write a quick blog, before it's back out on our bikes for some rock climbing, tree trekking and zip wiring.

Then after that, it's off into the huge pool complex for some moonlit, outdoor rapids and a ride on a family raft slide, followed by dinner at one of the many on-site restaurants, a night time cycle back to the cabin and a movie to end the day.

Everyone sleeps really well, probably from the unusual amount of exercise we do and all that fresh air, or perhaps it's the dark and stillness of the forest, but either way we always feel pretty rested the next day.

I never want to leave when our break comes to an end and I wish there was a way of incorporating all of this type of living into our everyday lives at home, where for a few days the phrase 'what's the WiFi code?' is forgotten, but somehow real life just gets in the way.

Oh well, I guess that's what makes a holiday a holiday, doing something you don't normally do, but I don't care how old the kids or I get, I'm going to keep coming back here 'til I'm 95. After all, they even have 4 wheeler bikes here which are basically motorised wheelchairs, so there really is no excuse!

APRIL 2017 – GRANDPARENTS HIT THE NET

An Old Recipe With A Difference

Ingredients:
1 x Septuagenarian
1 x Octogenarian
1 x Facebook Page

Method:
Mix all ingredients together for a surfing good 'ole party!

Notes:
I've learnt a new word today.

Me: Hi Google, what is the common term used for people over 70?

Google: Septuagenarian.

Me: Thanks Google, love you x

Google: Love you too x (ok that bit's a lie, but I like to imagine Google is my secret toy boy!)

So, with my new word firmly filed away into my very short-term memory, let me introduce you to my 77 year old Mum and 80 year old Dad.

My Mum has ALWAYS looked amazing. She is beautiful, very fashionable, petite and I've always been told she looks like my sister.

But you see, I'm not proud of her because of how she looks, I'm proud because my Mum (and my Dad) have NEVER acted their ages. EVER.

In fact growing up, there were often some REALLY embarrassing moments.

Like the time, aged 17, I invited my first ever boyfriend over to meet my parents and forgot they were both on their way out to a fancy dress party, hosted by the hospital my Dad was currently working at.

So, down the stairs comes a very sexy, green and red pixie 'girl' and a less sexy, green and red, odd looking bloke, with the sign: 'THE NATIONAL ELF' sellotaped to his slightly protruding belly!

OMG! The look on my boyfriend's face said it all, and sadly that relationship lasted all of 1 week.

But I don't blame my parents, it was his loss, he was the one missing out on all the fun, because our house was always the place to be for great parties.

My parents were the ones who hosted a big New Year's Eve party every year; walls clad with cut out adverts from newspaper magazines to play the 'guess the advert game', the prizes usually consisted of some type of alcohol.

There were bowls of mulled wine, which were eventually laced with various other mad concoctions; my Dad's medic friends always thought it would be fun to carry out some 'experiments' on the guests, all in the name of, ahem, 'science'.

Also lots of spontaneous karaoke sessions were to be had that finally managed to scare off our 'never to be seen again' cat, (who I presumed had got lost in the wilderness, but in reality was probably either given away as the main prize for the 'guess the advert game', or donated to the hospital lab for experimentation).

BUT, thankfully, there were at least no key swapping games (well, none that I was aware of anyway!)

Fast forward 30 years and I'm delighted to say my parents are still partying like there's no stopping them. They have both worked tremendously hard all their lives and have never had spare cash to spend on themselves, so it's wonderful to see them being able to do it now.

They are always going to the theatre, cinema, out for dinner, at an art gallery, playing bridge with friends, taking up new hobbies with or without the grandchildren. Sure, they've both had health problems over the last few years, but now they are thankfully ok, and they are living life to the full while they still can.

My Dad, as well as being a surgeon and an artist, has always loved technology. He's tried to keep up with the kids by setting up a Twitter and Facebook account, keeping in touch with colleagues all over the world, but I feared my Mum would be left behind.

She always loved writing, and people often said she should write a book one day, so it was about a month or two ago that I suggested to her that she set up a Facebook group for the over 70's; an extension of my group for the over 40's.

She thought it sounded fun and the name 'Gin & Fizz' was developed, inspired by her favourite tipple and it also seemed like a nice way to complement 'The Latte Lounge'.

So 'Top Tips 4 Women Over 70' began and we waited, and we waited for it to take off like my group had, we expected another 2,000 in 2 days to eagerly ask to join.

But, it soon became apparent that it was more likely to be 2 in 2 days, and we realised we had an interesting PR and marketing job on our hands if this was going to be successful.

You see, what neither of us had banked on was the fact that many over 70's are either not on Facebook or if they are, they don't know how to properly use it!

So when my Mum added a few of her friends to the group, with a lovely welcoming note to new members, the first comment had me wetting myself;

"What a great idea Judy, I'd love to be on your group, how do I do that?"

Bless her, Mum couldn't bring herself to say "You already are on this group, hence how you are able to comment."

It's been a slow but steady burn, with Mum posting really interesting articles, or writing about places she's been and she's had half a dozen members commenting or joining in, but it's taken time for them to realise that it's not her own personal blog and it's ok to ask for recommendations for a plumber, electrician or physio!

I think a lot of her friends would still rather use the Yellow Pages (does that still exist?) and don't really see the point of it. I guess what we've both realised now is that the over 40's all joined Facebook because our kids were on it, so it really seems to have, so far, skipped most of her generation.

However, Mum has never been one to give up on anything, and I'm really proud of how she has now got the knack of social media.

Luckily, my Dad is always in the background helping her upload images and news articles if she gets a bit confused, and I'm there to help her navigate the World Wide Web if she needs to, but I think it's going to take time to get the others properly on board.

Now with just over 300 members however, there is definitely something to be said for having a smaller group of like-minded women. It has a lovely village community feel to it right now and hasn't lost the personal touch.

So, as some of you or your parents graduate on from The Latte conversations and are ready for a bit of Gin and Fizz, well now know where to find it!

MAY 2017 – FITNESS FADS
50 Shades of Exercise

In my 30 year quest to keep fit, I think I have pretty much tried every exercise regime known to man; some with great success, others less so.

But my problem is, although I love exercise, I get bored quickly and deep down I'm actually quite lazy. I would far rather have a lovely sit down with a cup of tea and a good book than go to the gym (hence the current size of my backside!)

Although today, I have decided to try something new 'Reformer Pilates'. After all, anything that involves lying down on a bed whilst exercising has my name written all over it.

Well... all I can say is blimey! I thought I'd walked into The Red Room in 50 shades of Grey (yes, I did read it, totally fabulous trash!) I actually got a bit excited seeing all those straps, hooks and chains on a Tuesday morning, (I'm so middle aged).

Anyway, 55 mins later and although not a Christian Grey blindfold or whip in sight, I still came out smiling, exhausted, slightly stretched and feeling a bit wobbly on the ole legs!

It was a really fun experience and, as I left the group, I did wonder why I was getting some weird looks, but assumed it was just because I was new. It wasn't until I got home and looked in the mirror that I saw this massive hole in my leggings, ripped at the seam down my backside. I think the machine had stretched me and my bottom further than my lycra could cope with.

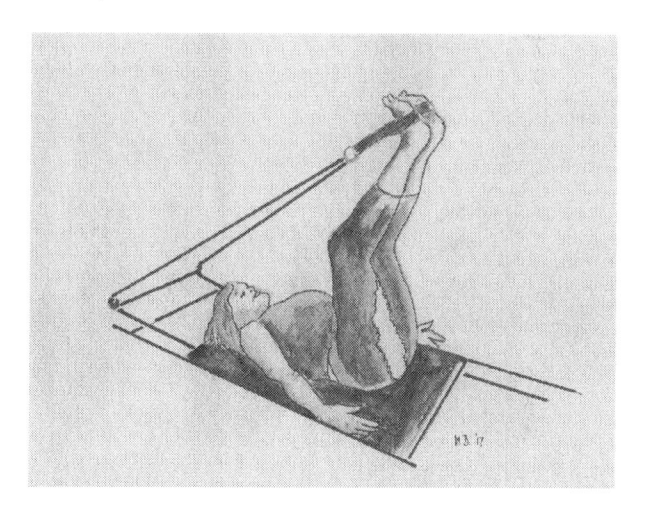

Oh dear, yet another place I'm going to have to avoid in my quest to keep my dignity intact.

JUNE 2017 – BACK TO WORK
'It's A Whole New World'

Wow! I've just stepped into (and skipped out of) some sort of parallel universe, where people sit on luminous green and pink chairs next to rows of purple and orange painted telephone boxes, in floor-to-ceiling glass offices, 10 stories high, (think Tellytubbies meets The Office).

I walk past lots of boys? Men? Hard to tell, but all dressed in jeans, sporting the same goaty beard with a glazed look in their eye, which I can only presume is from spending too much time working on digital start-ups.

I am reliably informed that this is where a very well-known social media platform works from, and I don't know why, but just by walking out of my very suburban home office, (well less office, more Mac on kitchen table!) and into this young and buzzing environment, it immediately fills me with excitement and possibility.

You see, for many mums like me who perhaps used to work for companies in a big city, pre-kids, you forget that the world has pretty much carried on without you.

You go about bringing up your kids, perhaps finding

part or full time work more locally to fit in around them, focusing more on how to 'fit it all in', 'make it work' and 'balance everything', but somewhere along the line you forget who you used to be.

And then you find yourself probably in your 40's, or 50's, and the kids don't need you as much and your own parents are so far doing fine without you, and you think, 'ok… now what?'

So today, as I went to meet some lovely ladies to discuss collaboration, I was reminded of the person I used to be, but was shocked at how much things have changed.

We didn't meet in a boardroom, or an office, but what they called 'The Kitchen'. Of course, this wasn't some grubby canteen, but a room with a very trendy Union Jack fridge and rows of long yellow desks, yellow benches, and plastic walls covered in post-it notes. This was obviously where these digital kids go to brainstorm and I loved it!!

So the reason for this blog is to say that sometimes, just sometimes, it is really good for the soul to step out of its comfort zone and remember who we used to be; that there is a whole world out there which we should all re-introduce ourselves to, be it for work, travel, new friends, new hobbies, anything.

As they say (not sure who <u>they</u> are? But…) IF YOU KEEP DOING THE SAME THINGS, YOU WILL GET THE SAME OUTCOME so, time to change it up a bit, and I now know where my new office is going to be!

And even though I'm not sure how well a middle aged, overweight woman would go 'down wiv de kids', they actually all look like they need a good meal, so perhaps I could come with chicken soup every day.

JULY 2017 – SOMETHING'S MISSING!

Where's my keys, where's my car, where's my memory?

Sometimes I worry that I'm developing early onset Alzheimer's.

This morning, I spent 20 minutes looking for my keys, which are always hanging up on the key holder rack above the radiator cover in the kitchen. But when I went to look this morning, they were nowhere to be seen. And even more annoyingly, someone had taken the eggs out the fridge and left them sitting on the radiator cover shelf, getting warm.

"When did you last have them," my husband asks helpfully.

"Yesterday at 4pm, when I picked the kids up from the tube after school," I reply.

"Oh," he says.

"Oh? How does that help me?" I snap back.

I rack my brains, think, think; I came in and threw my coat over the kitchen chair. Oh no... hang on, I remember I was desperate for the loo, so I go and check in there to see if I've put keys on the side of the toilet. Nope, ok. Where else? think, think. Ooooh, I know. I went to the loo then remembered I'd left my shopping in the car so must've gone back with my keys: Go to car, nope it's still locked.

Ok, where else? Brought shopping in, put food in fridge, close... oh fuck... and then it comes to me. I open the fridge slowly and yup there they are, my keys are on the shelf normally reserved for the eggs and the eggs are... UCH! Feel like such a bloody idiot, but no time for that, and no one need know.

Finally in car, rush kids to tube, slightly later than planned, then zoom off to Sainsbury's to stock up on provisions for the weekend. I decide to park outside Costa on the main road, to avoid wasting any time queuing to get out of the car park afterwards.

Plan is: Do a quick supermarket sweep so I can get back home to walk dog, let plumber in, tidy house, finish some work, prep dinner before its back to the tube for the 4pm pickup.

Ok, where's my car? I definitely parked it in the 3rd row of the carpark by the entrance. Little bright blue Fiat 500, can't miss it. I push my trolley all the way to the end smiling smugly that it's coming up any minute.

No? Shit. Ok, it must've been the 4th row, do a loop round and continue to push my trolley back feeling quite sure it will present itself to me any minute. FUCK FUCK FUCK! Where's my flippin' car? 5th row? NO, back to 2nd row. NO. NO. NO! Starting to break out into a hot sweat.

Oh for God's sake, where's my... OMG not again, suddenly it dawns on me, I parked it by Costa on the main road.

Turning to check no one has been watching me all this time, I race up the ramp to reclaim said little blue car and then run home and decide it may be time to make an appointment with a neurologist.

Whilst I'm 'holding' on the phone to the secretary, I desperately search the Apple iTunes app catalogue to see if anyone has invented an app for finding your keys and your car or even better, finding my memory.

AUGUST 2017 – HOLIDAY AT SEA

An Alternative View On Cruising, By a Virgin Cruiser

It's our first full day on a cruise at sea, and when most people are relieved to be sleeping in because there is no stopping, today I am up at 7am.

You see, I've been reliably informed that there are 3,500 people on board and only 1,500 deckchairs. So I'm on a mission, and for the sake of peace and sanity within my family unit, I'm out to bag the best chairs.

I arrive at Deck 16, the Solstice deck, a secret oasis of calm and tranquility away from 'Butlins-on-sea' (or Deck 14, as it is affectionately known).

Anyway, I triumphantly reserve 6 plush tangerine coloured double sunbeds on what I presume is deck 16, although it's hard to tell as it's still pitch black out.

A sun cream, a flip flop, a bus tour guide of Barcelona, some headphones, my beach bag and a sarong casually thrown over each chair to give the impression we've been there for hours (seriously, who am I fooling at this time of day?)

Ok, job done, my family are going to love me so

much I'm bursting with excitement. Oh no, hang-on, it's my bladder – shit, (literally), what to do?

My 4 babies and husband are fast asleep blissfully unaware of my dilemma. If I leave my sunbeds, they will remove all my belongings to allow another family to sit there.

Got it, I'll bribe the deck boy with a handful of euros and my very own rendition of 'I am sailing', a winning combo for sure.

He looks at me as if I am completely out of my mind (a fair assessment) and says,

"I will actually pay you to stop singing, Mrs," (rude). So I explain my dilemma and he assures me I can go and do my business, grab a coffee and be back within the allocated 30 mins slot before they start removing everything.

Phew, so 17 mins later (I had prunes last night), with my bowels emptied and my caffeine inhaled, I'm happily back to my suite of double beds and it's only 7.30am.

I feel as smug as James Bond after a successful mission, until it dawns on me that I now have to sit here for the next 4 hours with one eye open (in case the items on my other 5 chairs are removed), before any of my family actually wake up.

Oh well, it will be worth it for the hugs, high fives, medals and standing ovations that I definitely won't be receiving from my bunch of monosyllabic teenagers, not forgetting my long suffering husband who is surprisingly still by my side almost 24 mad years later.

Cruise Day 3

Oh my bloody God, not again! So I just got out of the shower and I'm standing stark naked in my cabin staring out of the open glass doors at the gorgeous view, when another cruise ship slowly goes by and everyone starts waving at me... so what do I do?

Yup, I waved back again! Why can't I just be normal and close the curtains!

I'm sure a few camera flashes went off too. (So if you see some mad, middle-aged, sunburnt, naked woman plastered all over social media anywhere, please do let me know!)

Can just imagine the Captain's commentary, "On our left we have Barcelona, and on our right we have..."

Last Day At Sea

It's 7.45am, I've allowed myself a 'sleep-in', as we now have 24 hours at sea before returning to our original destination, Port of Civittavetchi, Rome.

I take on the appearance of my 'casually strolling but secretly sprinting' walk to Deck 16 to reserve my chairs, but find I'm being pushed back by the strength of the gale force winds.

I'm determined to push through for the sake of my babies, grabbing onto the handrails in genuine terror that I might be casually tossed overboard and dumped into the deep, dark waters below.

Fifteen exhausting minutes later and I've made it. I feel and look like I've been in a tumble dryer on the quick spin cycle, and I plant my flagpole at the top of the solstice deck in celebration.

There are people lying here pretending to be asleep whilst grabbing onto the chairs for dear life. There are towels flapping around in the 'breeze', only now staying in place by some brightly coloured, no doubt Amazon-bought, deck chair towel clamps, and there are belongings strapped down to the deck with what looks like the rope attached to the ship's anchor.

Ok, I've got this: 6 deckchairs, 6 towels, no towel

clamps. If I lie down sideways across all 6 chairs, with my full weight (which is some weight after 10 days on board) and my legs spread-eagled, I can hold them in place whilst I (yet again) wait for my family to wake up.

I'm getting a lot of very strange looks, and to be quite honest, I'm sure I feel a few spots of rain...

Wtf?! Have I totally lost my mind? Screw this, screw them, this is meant to be a holiday, I'm going back to bed where it's warm, dry and I can lie down without risking my life.

So I won't get the medal today for 'hero sunbed reserving mum', but then again I didn't get it last week either!

It's been a really funny ole holiday, we've met some really lovely people, visited some really lovely places and have now become completely institutionalised.

I will miss you Deck 16 and all your inhabitants!

SEPTEMBER 2017 – FAREWELL DEAR WOMB

Hysterical Hysterectomy

"A WOMB WITH A VIEW" – Pre-op Diary

H MINUS 6 DAYS, FRIDAY

Someone has added me to a Facebook group called 'Hyster-Sisters', sounds very American and to be honest, I'm not sure whether this is a group for women undergoing hysterectomies or a group for hysterical sisters. Well, I guess my sister Suzanne and I both think we are hysterically funny at times, even when no-one else does, as well as being hysterical in a crazy sort of way, so regardless, this group intrigues me.

My stay on the group consists of approximately 12

and a half minutes. 10 minutes of reading about the enormous amounts of trapped wind I'm likely to encounter post op, and 2 and a half minutes trying to stop myself from throwing up while looking at all the various scars that some of the members want me to examine for fear of post-op infection.

I quickly remove myself from the group as it is beginning to put the fear of God into me.

H MINUS 5 DAYS, SATURDAY

Went to see the surgeon today to go through my worries and concerns, not sure his passing last words were particularly helpful, "Don't worry, I've never buried one yet!"

Been so busy with work and family that haven't had a calm moment to think about the op. Although starting to get butterflies now, just need to get on with it so I can get on with recovery.

H MINUS 4 DAYS, SUNDAY

Started googling all the negatives of having this procedure, and now in a total state of panic. Sent various articles to Dr Dad to examine whose response "What absolute bollocks" was just what I needed to hear. Note to self, stop reading things on line.

H MINUS 3 DAYS, MONDAY

Butterflies galore, so trying to keep busy all day. Clearing fridge, stocking up fridge, packing bags, unpacking bags, feels like I'm going in for a baby, instead of going in for them to remove the first ever home my babies ever knew. But on the plus side, my gorgeous oldest son has just arrived home from Uni after a long six weeks, which has been a huge boost to my pre-op nerves. So happy to see him.

H MINUS 2 DAYS-TUESDAY & HALLOWEEN

Just been for my pre-op assessment. Waited an hour for blood tests, she couldn't find a vein in either arm, or hand, but eventually got what she needed out of some random area.

She told me she was American and very big on Halloween, and then sweetly asked if she could keep some of my blood to use when she dressed up as Count Dracula later on, (I actually don't think she was joking!)

Upstairs to see the nurse:
Weight- omg are you having a laugh?
Blood pressure -low as ever.
Nose and groin swabs for MRSA (groin swabs?!)

We discuss the blood thinning injections that I'll

need to administer for the month afterwards, and the sexy, thigh-high DVT prevention stockings I'll need to wear 24/7. I did ask if they come in black leather, but apparently there isn't much call for them these days.

Discuss this bizarre side-effect of trapped wind. Apparently, if I lift my arms up post-op, the wind will travel up to my shoulders and dissipate somewhere. Not quite sure whether it then comes out of my ears, mouth or nose but to be honest, I'm not sure my poor husband will notice much difference anyway.

Went to cinema with oldest son early eve to see a real weepy 'pretend I'm crying about the film' in the dark, when really I just needed a good ole cry to release all these trapped emotions!!

H MINUS 1 DAY – WEDNESDAY

On the back of lots of recommendations, I have bought 5 pairs of massive 'Bridget Jones' knickers, peppermint tea bags, Mentos, double mints, Windeze, straws, cushioned tray table, cuddly toy and a presentation knife set (ok, well perhaps not the last two from the Generation Game, am I showing my age?)

Had a lovely lunch with oldest son, packed a few bits,

sorted out instructions for the house, kids, dog and hubby, watched Bake Off final then off to bed in nervous anticipation.

There are many women (including two of my very good friends) that have had to have this operation for far worse reasons than me, and I know they have both done it with immense bravery, so I am just going to count myself lucky, get my head down, get on with it and hopefully come out the other side a new woman (I've asked to be transformed into a supermodel if at all possible, but he laughed and said "I'm a doctor, not a magician- nice!)

THURSDAY H DAY

7am No sleep I rock up in my hospital chic wear (aka pjs, slippers and dressing gown) and for a minute it feels like I'm going on a mini break, pulling my overnight bag behind me.

My consultant reassures me he's only ever perforated 3 bladders in 30 years (this guys a joker!) then says I hear from the lady next door you run a women's Facebook group, (wonder whose next door?)

I blush and say, "Err... Yeah," to which he replies,

"Well, I better do a good job then or I'll be outta

work!'

He has 6 day cases before me so I won't be going down TIL around 10.30am, think I'm going to try and sleep.

Adios amigos, See you on the other side!

Womb Service – POST-OP DIARY

A long anxious wait in our room for 3 hours before it's time to go down. Kissing the hubby goodbye, I try to stay calm as I'm put to sleep. The miracle of modern analgesia; to wake up with no memory of anything happening. I hear someone say my name in recovery a few times, a warm touch on my hand says I'm fine and it all went well. I shed a little tear.

Wheeled back to my bedroom in a morphine induced state, I have no memory of this day at all, which is probably a good thing.

I think my Mum came to visit. Think I may have told the trolley porter I loved him.

November 3rd - Friday H Day +1

Still very sleepy and drugged up but feel no pain and being looked after by a gorgeous, bubbly, friendly nurse with a great sense of humour. Makes all the difference to your recovery when you feel well cared for and safe.

Catheter and oxygen tubes removed, various drips inserted, one hand doesn't like drip and blows up like a fat balloon so we swap to the other hand.

Nurse suggests that I sleep with fat hand raised on what she calls my 'princess pillow!'

No appetite, even though apparently I ordered a 3 course meal for today before I went down for op! (Shame, I love my food).

Beautiful flowers arrive from some of my pals which really cheered me up.

November 4th - Saturday H Day+ 2

Still no appetite, so breakfast tray sent away again.

The kids all pop in to visit -2 are on their way to our local shopping centre, Brent Cross, one delaying the impending revision session and the other off to a matinee with his Grandpa. Miss them all like mad, especially as big two at Uni, so nice to see them all together chatting away as friends, makes me happy and proud.

Nurse takes out stomach drain, horrible feeling but I'm relieved it's out. Drip taken down too, so at least I'm now detached from everything.

Best friend and her hubby come to visit with a gorgeous lap-tray covered with photos of my puppy Bobbie; such a thoughtful gift and really cheered me up as I'm missing my dog like mad.

Sister comes to visit with lovely toiletries, magazines and of course some more mints. She says she's made lots of food for when we get home; my hubby and kids could get used to this, I certainly could!

I've managed to eat for the first time; a baked potato and cheese with salad. They're hoping we can get a bowel movement going (tmi?!)

Hubby comes back with my laptop for a Saturday night's viewing of 'Stranger Things'. Only manage one episode before I fall asleep again at 9pm.

November 5th - Sunday Fireworks Night H Day +3

Was in a deep sleep until 7am, when I get woken up with the bang of a door being slammed open for 'womb service'.

"Morning, got you a fresh jug of water," the cheery male breakfast attendant shouts. He may as well have used a foghorn, it was so loud I jumped out of my skin, definitely not good for my stitches.

Feeling blue this morning for the first time, the

wound pain is sore, I guess I'm feeling it now that I'm morphine free. Desperately want to be home but they won't let me out until I've done a number 2.

Parents come to visit again, ex-surgeon Dad proclaims it's the most beautiful scar he's seen in a long time! Takes me for a walk up the corridor whilst holding onto his elbow reminds me of walking down the aisle with him 24 years ago, except this time I'm looking far less attractive in my nightie and slippers.

They sit around discussing their worries about Corbyn and reading the weekend papers, but all I'm thinking is 'where's the nurse with my suppository, I need to go'.

Foghorn man has just returned asking for my lunch request (I didn't dare tell him my real request -to be woken up a little more gently next time!)

Doctor has just been in and is very pleased with me. He says that if I can't go to the toilet naturally, I have two other options; corkscrew or forceps. (It's a laugh a minute here with my new favourite surgeon!)

He also doesn't want me to take to my bed when I'm home, but to walk to the newsagent and buy a Mars Bar (well, ok, think I can manage that!)

Hate that I'm missing Bonfire Night, always been one

of my favourite nights of the year, but my doctor says he is expecting fireworks in the toilet later and then I can go home, so gotta look at the positives!

Anyway, I'm sure I've shared far too much toilet humour and personal information in here, but I hope in some way it will help other women who have this op coming up. Please be reassured, the fear before is certainly not the reality, you will be fine!

(Ps. A huge shout out to my amazing hubby Hugh, who has finally learnt what multi-tasking is!)

OCTOBER 2017 – BACK TO THE FUTURE

Can We Talk Retro?

So, call it bad family planning, but 3 of my teenage kids birthdays all fall in the same week in October. Anyway, whilst I've been in hospital, they have been happily spending their birthday money on new clothes and various other bits and bobs, which I hadn't had the pleasure of seeing until yesterday.

"Mum, do you like my new vintage jumper?"
"Mum, what do you think of this retro jacket?"
"Mum, OMG! You have to see my classic cowboy boots."

And so began last night's fashion show whilst I sat watching, still very much recuperating, in my recliner chair.

Well blow me down! They've only gone and spent good money on all my old gear from the '80's, which to be honest was a bit naff even then. If I look hard enough, I will probably be able to track down the originals somewhere in a bag in the loft for free.

Since when did brown and mustard Pringle become retro? What makes a denim jacket suddenly vintage? And cowboy boots a classic?

One of them even had enough to buy a record player

with a very familiar collection ranging from Pink Floyd, David Bowie and Prince to ELO, Michael Jackson and Duran Duran.

Another had just come back from Uni clubbing on an '80's night, which was apparently so retro I wouldn't understand.

Also, we are all watching "Stranger Things" on Netflix at the moment, a cross between ET, Close Encounters of the 3rd Kind and Jurassic Park where kids race along on BMX bikes, with ridiculous mullets, chasing creepy beings!

OK hang on just one minute, what is going on? Did the surgeon knock me out and somehow transfer me via the DeLorean back to the future?! When did the '80's suddenly become cool again? I'm sorry, I was a teenager in the '80's and never once thought 'oh, I'm living in such a cool era, one day this will all become so 'in' again'.

And yet, their wardrobes remind me of a time when I was practicing my snogging routine with my pillow (pretending it was George Michael), wearing neon fingerless gloves with leg warmers to match, dreaming of being in Kids from Fame and what's more, knew every word from every song of my idol Madonna!

Yet I can remember all that, and I can't remember where I put my keys or why I just came into this room.

Oh well, I better go find my rara and puffball skirt and then dig out the ole shoulder pads just in case.

Mind you, having said all that, I'm not sure my 3 sons would particularly rock that look!

NOVEMBER 2017 – MEN HUH?
Whoaaaa!

Let's get one thing straight, I've never thought of myself as a staunch feminist and certainly not a man-hater. In fact, I love most men.

I love my husband and my 3 teenage boys, I love my Dad and my brother Richard and my male friends and relatives.

But, sometimes, I do laugh at how these poor blokes deal with 'women's issues'.

I even feel sorry for them. We really are, at times, incredibly difficult to read/ handle/ understand… but this weekend I experienced a first for me.

I was sitting next to one of these much loved 'male species' at a party, who wasn't aware I had recently had an operation and he enquired as to how I was. I said I was fine, just a bit tired post-op, to which he replied,

"Oh? What did you have done?"

I guess it didn't occur to me that some men may not know how to respond to the reply;

"I've just had a hysterectomy."

I assumed it would follow with the words 'oh dear, I'm sorry, that's not pleasant, hope you are doing ok?'

But instead, and I kid you not, he physically recoiled, backed off with his hands in the air saying "Whooaaaa". He then proceeded to look thoroughly embarrassed, before quickly going on to examine the pesky napkin that had somehow fallen off his lap and onto the floor!

I decided to help him out of this 'awkward' situation by standing up and pretending to see an old friend I hadn't seen in ages,

"Samanthaaaaaaaaa!!" I waved crazily, then quickly excused myself and waddled over to embrace... well, not her obviously. I actually ducked into the toilet before he had come up for air after retrieving his 'napkin'!

The thing is, I'm so used to being open with my friends about hormones, and periods and the 'ins and outs' of our bodily functions, that sometimes I forget there are perhaps a lot of people who when out and about, prefer to keep things a little more private.

It seems Breast Feeding, Menopause, Periods, Hormones and Hysterectomies are still very embarrassing and taboo subjects for our 'delicate' male friends, and so it is perhaps in hindsight best left to a night out with the girls, rather than thrown into the middle of a dinner party conversation.

So the next time my male friends ask me what's wrong, I think I will just say I broke my ankle to stop them from running out of the room for a 'family emergency'!

Actually, scrap that and replace with: 'Oh for God's sake, why don't you just go and grow a pair!'

Husband Trade-Off

"I'll walk the dog, if you wash up all of last night's dishes."

Those were the words I was greeted with by my husband, as I got out of bed this morning after a nice Saturday morning lie-in. Well, if you call 7.30am a lie-in.

"I'm sorry, how is that fair?" I retort, "how is walking a dog for half an hour in the fresh air, equal in both time and enjoyment levels to me standing at the sink washing up last night's dinner plates?" (Dishwasher broken, by the way!)

"Fine. I'll do the dishes, you walk the dog," he says.

"Deal." I say, (he wasn't expecting that!) "and I tell you what, I will open the curtains and make the bed and you can put the bins out."

"Oh for god's sake. I always put the bins out, why is that a man's job?"

"Fine. I'll put the bloody bins out and you make the bed and open the curtains."

"Fine, deal," he replies very sarcastically.

And so the deals go on all day, all week; we trade-off jobs and responsibilities for the house, for the kids, for our work and parents. We even debate who bought the latest pint of milk, battery, light bulb or cinema ticket.

We've never actually stopped and examined why we do this, or indeed if each trade off really is equal to the other, but when you stop and look at it, it's actually very funny.

So here is my list of usual trade-offs in our house, feel free to add you own!

"FINE I'LL...	IF YOU..."
PUT BINS OUT	ACTUALLLY PUT THE RUBBISH IN THE BIN,
DO LAUNDRY	PICK UP THE LAUNDRY OFF THE FLOOR
WASH AND DRY DISHES	WASH AND DRY DOG
WALK DOG	IF YOU WALK FULL STOP
DROP KIDS	IF YOU REMEMBER TO PICK UP KIDS
MAKE DINNER	IF YOU PUT PLATES ACTUALLY IN THE SINK, NOT NEXT TO IT
CALL YOUR PARENTS	CALL MINE
DO ANYTHING	SLEEP WITH ME EVER!

DECEMBER 2017 – RIGHT ON WOMEN

Putting The Feminine Back In Feminism

Sometimes I write a word or two in a blog, without thinking about the way it can be misinterpreted, or even perhaps read as offensive, incorrect or unhelpful.

When I do this, I'm genuinely grateful to be made aware of my mistake and picked up on it accordingly, which is what happened when I offended someone with the wrong use of the word 'feminism' and put it side-by-side with the phrase 'man-hater'.

You see, growing up, my view on the word 'feminism' was actually quite negative. To me it represented a lot of angry women on the TV, stamping their feet and demanding to be treated like a man.

Yes, of course, I'm eternally grateful to all the suffragettes who fought for us to have the right to vote amongst other things, and it is horrendous to see and read about all the sexual harassment that women have to put up with, both in their personal lives and their working lives.

So perhaps I'm either being a bit naïve, or I'm just lucky, but I've never been treated badly or differently in my career. I've always spoken up if I felt I was being treated unfairly, and been given respect where it was due by my male colleagues and given equal pay accordingly.

I don't want to be treated like a man, I like being a woman and feminine. Yes, I do not want to be groped or harassed, and yes I do believe in equal pay, but I get very upset when I see many women who use it as a phrase to basically hate and bash men.

I love most men and what I tried to illustrate in my blog was that sometimes, I forget how far we still have to go with men being comfortable talking about women's personal stuff.

I love the man I was talking about in my blog. I felt sorry that I'd embarrassed him when discussing my recent hysterectomy op and it made me realise that actually, we don't need to necessarily talk about lots of very personal stuff in a public place!

I used to work for a mental health charity, so I'm all

for talking about mental health issues and breaking the menopause taboo, in the press and amongst girlfriends/GPs or educating male bosses in the work place to be more understanding and supportive. But when it comes to talking about the 'ins and outs' of the female body, in other social situations perhaps with some warning!

My husband is very supportive about my menopause journey and has learnt a lot about it. So I'm trying to bring my boys up normalising it. Always easier working on the younger generation rather than trying to change how a group of older men will react, it's probably too late for that, most older men are sadly quite stuck in their ways!

I talk to my daughter all the time about being confident in who she is and what she believes in, that she should speak up for herself and what she wants, but equally not batter men into submission to get it. If you are a fair and likeable, honest woman, who asks for what she wants, I'd like to think/hope that, usually in most situations, you will be heard.

Obviously my background is in Communications in the Third Sector, so very different from perhaps banking/law etc. but I just feel that a bit of compassion, from both sexes, goes a long way.

The old use of the word 'feminism' in my mind, has negative connotations and personally I think it needs to change from being seen as an angry bunch of overbearing 'right-on' women, to something more appropriate.

So, although I am sorry for any offense caused, I personally think a change of terminology may go a long way. Or, a good PR campaign;

Let's keep the 'feminine' in feminism!

~ end ~

THE LATTE LOUNGE FACEBOOK GROUP 2017 YEAR IN REVIEW

JANUARY

We start the year hitting 4,000 members.

The Latte Lounge Group is discussed on The Vanessa Feltz Radio Show.

FEBRUARY

Members kindly donated lots of valentine presents from their businesses for me to distribute to some lucky members.

MARCH

Members very generously gave me some free prizes from many of their businesses to give away to some of our members during a Mother's Day promotion.

APRIL

Members offered masses of discounts and promotions from their businesses for other members to enjoy.

MAY

The JC Newspaper features the background story to The Latte Lounge Group.

Work begins on The Latte Lounge website.

JUNE

We celebrate the group's first birthday and hit 6,000 members.

We enjoyed our 2nd Latte Lounge charity retreat day and raised hundreds of pounds for The Daisy Network.

Website medical committee and bloggers group formed.

JULY

Teachers gifts free weekends of ads introduced.

Website team of bloggers first meeting held.

AUGUST

We hit 7,000 members.

Summer sandals giveaway competition.

SEPTEMBER

We launch Charity Tuesday.

Website digital partner/s agreed.

OCTOBER

Fabulous Magazine (The Sun Newspaper) features The Latte Lounge Group.

We link our Group to The Menopause Support Network and Gin & Fizz (Top Tips 4 Women Over 70!)

NOVEMBER

Members came together and nominated their favourites charities and donated over 60 prizes for our online auction. We raised over £1,200 for Chai Cancer Care.

DECEMBER

We hit 10,000 members.

We celebrate 'Small Business Saturday'.

The Latte Lounge Group is discussed on BBC Radio London.

We launch Friday 'Trade for a Trade' Day.

We throw in Free Ads every Sunday for the festive season.

AND WE HAVE:

Recommended everything from Dr's and dentists to builders and bakers.

Found, or offered, members and their children jobs or work experience opportunities.

Enjoyed a year's worth of free advertising.

Offered members some amazing discounts.

Shared personal stories and interesting articles in the media.

Helped many women in distress and signpost them on to the right agencies.

Joined in the trending conversations from 'World Menopause Day' to 'International Mental Health Day', and so many other relevant calendar days/weeks and months in-between!

BUT MOST OF ALL, WE HAVE COME TOGETHER AS A COMMUNITY AND SHOWN THAT US OLDER WOMEN ARE STRONG, WARM, CARING, KIND, GIVING, FRIENDLY, HELPFUL, BRIGHT AND ABOVE ALL, A BLOODY GOOD LAUGH!

Printed in Great Britain
by Amazon